10 Mistakes Startup Businesses Make & How You Can Avoid Them

A written piece by Dee Edwards

COPYRIGHT:

Dee Edwards Publishing, Trussville, AL

Copyright The Startup Business Factory, 2016

All rights reserved. No part of this book may be reproduced in any form without written permission form the author. Reviewers may quote brief passages in review.

Published 2016

DISCLAIMER

No part of this publication may be reproduced or transmitted in any form or by any means, mechanical or electronic, including photocopying or recording, or by an information storage and retrieval system, or transmitted by email without permission in writing from the author.

Neither the author nor the publisher assumes any responsibility for errors, omissions, or contrary interpretations of the subject matter herein. Any perceived slight of any individual or organization is purely unintentional.

Brand and product names are trademarks or registered trademarks of their respective owners.

Acknowledgments

I give honor to God for being the one who created me with purpose—for using someone like me who has made many mistakes and for using me when others had written me off. I know you allowed me to go through many trials to lift me up before man so that you may be glorified. Thank you for handpicking me.

With tears in my eyes, I want to thank my husband for always supporting me. Words cannot explain how much I appreciate your support and how you have allowed me to simply be me. Every time you say, "Baby, I'm proud of you," it gives me motivation to keep pressing and pushing.

To my children, Michael and Aubrey, who have pushed me to become better every single day, you're my *why*. I love you to the moon and back. I hope your dad and I constantly make you proud.

I am very grateful for my Pastor and First Lady, Michael and Angela McClure, for believing in a broken girl who walked through the doors of your church. I have been a thorn in your side since I was twenty-three years old, but you've always been patient with me, served as an example and been loving toward me. Thank you for not giving up.

To all my friends: Lord knows you make me better. Every last one of you have been exactly what I needed in my life, and

I appreciate all the prayers and support you have shown me through the years. Thank you Lolita D., Nachandra, Kristalyn, Crystal P., Ranelli W., Brandy, India, Eboni, Lola, Tracy W., Toya M., Janica, Crystal N., Cadeshia, S., Maleatra, Dee, Melva T., Curtis R., Marcus, Jennifer T., and many others who I know I'm going to get in trouble for leaving out. Blame old age and not my heart. Thank you to everyone who believed in me and motivated me and pushed me to become better.

Tae, you deserve a special section all to yourself. All I can say is that I love you, and every single day you prove your love and friendship to me. You're such a wonderful friend and business acquaintance. You're constantly looking for ways to support me and help me without asking for anything in return. You have truly shown me what it means to be a friend. Thank you, thank you, thank you for your loyalty. Friendship like yours are hard to come by.

Thank you to Aprille Franks-Hunt, Master Business Coach of Coach, Speak and Serve for challenging me to write this book. My time with you has ignited a flame that will never die.

Allison Arnett, thank you for your support in making my dream come true. You are definitely the Creative Accountant.

Felicia Phillips, Business Strategist of Pinkpreneur, you are definitely serving a purpose in my life and business. Thank you. To my wonderful sister, Connie Washington, you always talk about how much I aspire you, so maybe if you see it in writing you will understand how much you mean to me.

Thank you for igniting the fire in me to wholeheartedly pursue my dreams.

To my parents, Donnie and Georgetta Evans, thank you for creating me. You could have aborted me, but you didn't. Because of you, I can walk in purpose.

To my church family, The Celebration Church, thank for your kind words and allowing me to lead you and pursue my purpose without judgment.

None of this would be possible if it wasn't for my boss whom I looked up to who made the final decision to fire me. Thank you. Many would say I'm acknowledging her because I am bitter. No, I'm acknowledging her because she listened to God. Her obedience was a setup to bring me to this place of success.

What Others Are Saying

Building a successful business is like building a structurally sound house. It all starts with a strong foundation. Dee's advice would have saved me countless hours and thousands of dollars if this book was around when I started my business nearly 20years ago. Excellent tips for the individual ready to #PutInTheWork to launch or up-level their business. A must read for sure.

Melva Tate, PHR/CLC | Consultant | Coach | Speaker

Dee Edwards has discovered the keys to success and used it to unlock, unveil and unfold the mysterious truths to starting a business from ground level zero. Regardless of your stage, status, or stand in life, the words that are printed on the pages of this book will give readers the necessary tools needed to make your dream a reality. In closing, I've found the real power behind the pages of this book is the fact that the author has actually walked out, step-by-step, every word she writes to become the Fiery, Focused, Fruitful and Faithful entrepreneur she has become. Enjoy reading this book, do it twice, maybe even three times.

I'm Mike McClure & I approve this message. Senior Pastor of Revelation Church

Too many entrepreneurs today are running their businesses as hobbies and don't even know it. If you want a clear guide to steer you in the right direction, then you must read this book. Dee spells out for you how the IRS determines if you are operating a business or just managing a hobby. She also provides specific steps you need to take in order run a successful business. This is a must read. You cannot build a legacy on a hobby.

Ranelli Williams, CPA | Faith & Legacy Building Catalyst

I absolutely love this book. Dee Edwards gives an unfiltered truth to entrepreneurship. By eloquently mixing factual information with real examples of day-to-day challenges, it allows the reader the opportunity to process how to avoid innocent mistakes made by new and even advanced business owner. This is a must read for anyone looking to start a business.

Felicia Phillips, Founder The PINKpreneur Network & Master Business Strategist

What an amazing resource for all aspiring business owners! The straight forward honest tone with which Dee writes will inspire any budding entrepreneur to put forth their best effort to make their business a success. The breakdowns that she provide for each topic, as well as the supporting information from the IRS give easy to follow instructions on how to distinguish your business from a hobby, and ultimately generate a profit. In true Dee fashion, the openness with which she speaks makes her relatable to those aspiring to reach her level of success.

Kristalyn Lee, Director of Executive Affairs & Liaison to the Board of Trustees at University of Montevallo

Foreword

Small business leaders are the cornerstone of any community, and Dee Edwards is one of many who is determined to make a difference in the lives of entrepreneurs and her community.

When I first met Dee, just by mere conversation, I knew she had the heart to capture the essence of individuals to succeed in their businesses. She understands that business ownership is the driving force for building substantial wealth, and it is her vision to help entrepreneurs experience financial freedom.

This book is like having your opponent's playbook with their ten plays. Dee has gracefully taken the time to compile the helpful and useful information that is going to position entrepreneurs to win. So, find your quiet space, grab your highlighter, pen, and pad, and apply.

School is now in session.

Curtis K. Richardson,

www.cjelectricalservice.com/profile.html
State Licensed, ALDOT Certified
MBE/ DBE(BCIA), BAA Certified

Table of Contents

Acknowledgments iii

Foreword viii

Dedication xi

Introduction 1

Mistake #1 - Starting a Business Solely on Passion 9

Mistake #2 - Not Investing In Yourself 14

Mistake #3 - Running Your Business as a Hobby 23

Mistake #4 - No Proof. No Trail 38

Mistake #5 - Mixing Business & Personal Funds 45

Mistake #6 - No Plan. No Pay 53

Mistake #7 - Limiting Your Income Potential 59

Mistake #8 - Prideful, Not Asking For Help 63

Mistake #9 - Separating You from Your Business 71

Mistake #10 - Lack of Consistency 78

Final Thoughts 85

Dedication

To My Fellow Entrepreneurs,

You may have taken your last dollar, borrowed against your house, maxed out your credit cards, withdrew from your 401(k) or cleared out your savings to start your business, and it seems as if it has been the worse decision of your life. However, it really proves how much you believe in your vision. In order to start a business, you have to believe in your own abilities to make it succeed, although you may be frustrated with the process.

Actually, you're in a good place to rise above your obstacles. I know firsthand that when you're down to nothing, your back is against the wall and you have utilized all of your resources, you have just positioned yourself to do your best work and come out stronger and wiser than you ever did going in. You're going to look back on the nights you cried, prayed, and wondered how you were going to make it, and those memories are going to be your testimony to help other business owners. Stop second guessing yourself. The dream has been planted inside of you; therefore, you are equipped with everything you need to build a profitable and sustainable business. If you work hard, operate in integrity, surround yourself with likeminded individuals, remain humble and are willing to learn, implement, and serve others, what you're craving will happen sooner rather than later. When you are about to give up, remember who motivates you to succeed.

This year has been my reminder of how important it is for me to trust my process. On June 5th, as I was getting ready for church, I received a phone call from my father, who had lost his wife of over 20 years 6 months prior, was in the emergency room. At the time, I wasn't alarmed, because for a few months he had been having extreme pain in his back, legs and stomach. Never in a million years would I have expected the next phone call to change my life. He had been diagnosed with stage 4 cancer that had spread to his liver and both lungs. Afterward, my father made the decision to move in with us; and, my husband and I took on the selfless act to become his full-time caretakers. If this situation would have happened a few years ago, we would have been in a panic. We would have been worried about finances, job security, vacation days, and how we were going to be available for my father. However, being in our purpose, following our dreams, and being entrepreneurs, prepared us to be able to emotionally, mentally, spiritually, and financially support him and provide him with room and board. So if you ever wondered why it's important to be in your purpose, let me give you two good reasons: you never know what the future holds and who will need you to be ready to catch them when life throws them a curve ball.

Initially you may not understand your purpose, but don't sit still. Get started doing what you know how to do and the rest will come together. Sometimes when a vision is given to us, we wait too long to move on it. We become discouraged or overwhelmed by the thought of getting started that we delay the process. For this reason alone, find a way to get started with your business now. You've wasted more than enough time thinking about being a business owner and seeing yourself doing it. Maybe you've been paralyzed by your very own action. Enough is enough. It's time to unleash the beast. Get in purpose and pursue.

So, before you give up, try it again a different way, and hopefully, this guide along with systems and strategies will help you become a better businessperson. Remember when all you have is a plan A, then giving up is *never* an option.

See You at the Top,

Introduction

When it's time to embark on your journey to entrepreneurship, it will be undoubtedly one of the most fearful moments of your life, yet it will be the most freeing decision you've ever made. If I didn't decide to start my business, I would have been miserable and turned into a complaining and bitter woman who continued to go from job to job blaming everyone for my unhappiness. Being out of purpose, I would have limited my income potential, and I would have been asking myself, "What if?" When you're not operating in purpose, you struggle to find your inner peace and happiness. Sometimes you can't sleep, things don't come together like they should. You're sad when you want to be happy. Things just won't seem right even though it may look right to others. All because you know you're outside of purpose.

You may be reading this guide and feeling as if you're stuck or you're too old to pursue your dreams, but there isn't a time frame on your success. Many of the most successful celebrities we celebrate today didn't pursue their dreams until their later years. Harlan Sanders, better known as Colonel Sanders of Kentucky Fried Chicken, was sixty-six when he began promoting his style of cooking and built an empire. Julia Childs, an international successful chef, did not enroll in culinary school until the age of thirty-six. These are just two examples that dreams don't expire.

It may take longer to get started than some, but do it anyway, even if it hurts. Oftentimes, the unknown paralyzes us from moving forward and we delay our own process. Not people. Not God. We do. Whatever is holding you back, release it and walk in faith. You're going to make mistakes. Don't shy away from them. Use them. You're not perfect. You're going to make plenty of errors along the way. It's part of your process. I made many mistakes and failed seemingly many times, but I made it here. Look at what happened with the mistakes that I've made: I used them to write this book. Find a way to use what you go through as a means and tools to help others.

Building your business is all up to you. No one is going to do the work or believe in you as much as you do. As a matter of fact, don't get upset if others aren't as passionate about it as you are. It's your vision. No one is going to see it the way you do. Others may not understand why you're working so hard, and it's not up to them to understand. The dream is YOURS and it has been planted in YOUR heart and that's all the validation you need. Focus on the outcome. Your end results. And allow that to be your motivation to continue to work harder each day until you unlock your wealth.

Use the obstacles that you face as stepping stones to turn obstacles into stepping stones. Remember:

1. **The race isn't given to the swift but to those who endure to the end.** Building a successful business is

about endurance. Many start, but many won't last. As a runner, endurance is strengthened by continuing to practice and push to be better than the last run. As a business owner, every day you're getting stronger and wiser than the day before, and you're building endurance.

2. **The vision is for an appointed time.** As a farmer has to go through a season of plowing and cultivating the grounds in order to harvest from his seeds, the same can be true for a business owner. All the hard work you're putting into your business are seeds you can expect to harvest in due season.

3. **Write the vision and make it plain.** When the thought or idea is written on the tablet of your heart, it is a dream. When it's written on paper, it becomes vision. Writing out your thoughts and ideas will help you have a clear view of what you're trying to achieve.

4. **Remember why you started.** When you want to quit, remember why you started. Memorize it. Quote it. Write it down and look at it, then find the motivation to get back in the fight and keep going. You may take a pause, but don't quit.

As a business owner, you will face many challenges in the startup phase that will make you want to throw in the towel, question your ability to build a profitable and sustainable business, or you will become stuck. It's all part of the process.

So if you're discouraged and on the verge of giving up, welcome to the part of the journey that every entrepreneur face.

My husband and I have been entrepreneurs since 2008; unfortunately, we have felt the same way too. It's the benchmark and curve in business that many startups don't survive. But you have a choice: figure it out or quit. In my entrepreneurship venture, we have owned or currently own real estate, a daycare, a courier service, a shoe store, a tax and financial firm, a tax school, a printing company, a janitorial service, a coaching firm for tax preparers and new entrepreneurs and a non-profit organization, so can you imagine the challenges we have had to face with starting our businesses? And not to mention, the pressure of having to prove to ourselves that we can do it and prove to others as a small business owner that we have what it takes to move from idea to execution—all while having the weight of the internal pressure placed upon us to succeed. Even when it felt as if everyone around us was surpassing us and moving forward, and our dream became seemingly stagnant, we knew that we had come too far to quit.

In 2008, my husband was fired from his job and I was fired from my job in 2012. All our security was gone. We had no other choice but to shut up and do the work as my friend, Stephanie Synclair would say. Being on an employer's payroll, you can expect to receive a paycheck at the end of the pay period, but being a full-time business owner is totally different from working a nine-to-five job. Many times you don't start your business with insurance, vacation days, sick time and the other luxuries from a job. It takes boldness and sacrifice to pursue your vision, and even more confidence to leave a corporate job to pursue your passion. We had to increase our momentum and realize our "why" behind our desire to succeed. When we initially started out in business all we wanted to do was to survive from one month to the next. Who would have thought that one idea would birth other streams of income that allows both of us to work as full-time entrepreneurs?

I remember working many long hours and investing energy, time, and all my family's assets into a business that I didn't know was going to succeed. I stayed up many nights pacing the floor, crying, and wondering if stepping out on faith was worth it. As I look back on my decision to obey the internal voice that was pushing me to launch into the unknown, I realize how determined I was to make my business work. I really didn't have any other choice—I didn't have a plan B. It was time for me to jump; it was either now or never. Who would have known that our efforts and using the solutions in this guide would allow us to hit our six figure mark in 2012?

I previously worked as a high school college recruiter—my dream job—and quickly moved up in the company, generating almost a six figure income. I went from a $39k annual salary to receiving a twenty-one percent raise within six months of employment, and my hard work and effort were consistently shown in bonuses and increases. While building continuous success in my previous position, I discovered I was pregnant with my first biological child after losing four babies. During this complicated time, I was placed on bedrest early on in my pregnancy, and while I thought my job was secure, I was fired as soon as my FMLA time expired. I went from building my second home, driving my dream car and having the career of my dreams to not knowing how my husband and I were going to take care of our nine-year-old son, whom I love as my own, Michael, and our newborn baby, Aubrey. With the support of my awesome husband, we put literally everything we had into our courier service and online retailer business, and by all means necessary, we had to make it work.

My husband and I have spent savings, blood, sweat, and tears trying to figure out ways to grow our business and avoid pricey mistakes. We soon discovered why many people start but only a small percentage endure the hardship and trials of being a new business owner. No one told us how perplexing it is as a startup business owner to build a profitable business and how much I would have to change my mindset in order to survive in the world of entrepreneurship. But I made it.

After eight long years, I've finally uncovered the keys to building a profitable business, and I'm ready to share with you what I've learned from this journey.

Growing up, my mom would tell me not to do certain things, but most of the time, I did them anyway. I had to pay for those mistakes and decisions because I wouldn't heed her teachings, but she tried to warn me that my actions would cause me to pay more than I was willing to, and she was right. In business, if you train yourself to listen and learn from the errors of others, you wouldn't have to spend time trying to figure out the answers to areas that others have already conquered. You can start the business of your dreams and bypass unnecessary mistakes that newbies make in your sought-out industry if you're willing to learn and apply. Otherwise, you could end up like me, always in trouble and regretting my decisions because I wouldn't listen to my mother.

What you have to offer is way too valuable for you to make avoidable mistakes due to a lack of knowledge or uncertainty. Sometimes we only get one chance to get it right. As a business owner, if you're serious about getting your business on the road to success or started in the right direction, you're on the right path by reading this book of solutions, *10 Mistakes Startup Businesses Make & How You Can Avoid Them*. I encourage you to finish this book. Whether you have been in business for a while or you've just started on this journey, every business owner will have at least one aha moment while reading this book.

The most successful business owners are those who try to avoid as many costly mistakes as possible, and they know how to learn from others. When I started on my journey to entrepreneurship, who would have known that having a great idea is not enough to turn it into a profitable business. Boy, did I make some costly mistakes. There's a price for mistakes that many aren't willing to pay. As a business owner, mistakes have great potential to hinder your ability to grow your business into a thriving company.

Surprisingly, many new entrepreneurs close their business(es) within eighteen months after making some of the top ten business mistakes discussed on the following pages. After reading this guide, it is my hope that you rethink and redo the way you do business forever.

Breathe in and breathe out, grab a pen and a notebook, and let the journey began.

Mistake #1 -Starting a Business Solely on Passion

If I were to ask you today by a show of hands, if you are starting your business based on passion, then like many others, you would probably raise both hands and say yes. According to the IRS, a business is the purchase and sales of goods in an attempt to make a profit – not in an effort to make passion. Things that I'm passionate about I give away or provide as a free service. If you are interested in providing a free service or product, your interest may be more in a non-profit organization than a business. Your company requires profit to survive. Let's say it together: Start with Passion, Thrive with Profit. Business success is defined by profit. Many business owners are too focused on what they want to do, how they want to do it, and when they want to do it that they forget about the clients' needs. This leads to bankruptcy and closures for many businesses.

Passion is a great motivator to get started in business; however, you need more than passion to stay in business. Or at least, allow passion to be the power source behind your method to create immense success in your business. To survive in business, do not be afraid to create goals that lead to creating the financial freedom that was initiated by passion, but you need profit to endure. Now the real question is, how can you help more people while generating the cash flow that you need to sustain your life and business and fulfill your passion?

The answer is simple: turn your passion into a profitable business that serves your clients. Have you heard of *Shark Tank*? It is a must-watch reality show for all business owners and entrepreneurs. *Shark Tank* features a panel of potential investors called "Sharks" who consider offers from aspiring entrepreneurs seeking investment for their business or products. The Sharks invest their own money into the business if they are interested in making a deal. When seeking to negotiate the deal, they are looking to invest in ventures that will generate them continuous profits. The Sharks can immediately identify one that can produce profit. After watching the show, I realize that the investors are really interested in businesses that have already made a substantial amount of profit and have the potential to grow steadily. When passion is discussed, it is paired with the owner's ability to convince the Sharks that with proven results that the business is scalable and can continue to grow beyond what the entrepreneurs have done within their own efforts.

Passion isn't solely about how it makes you feel. It's about evoking an emotion from the buyer. Now, don't get me wrong, you must have an interest in what you're offering, but sell to others what they are passionate about. When we started our online shoe store, Strictly Heels, people bought from my husband and me because *they* loved shoes. We sold to our clients what they were passionate about – shoes. Sell passion.

I opened up my boutique to fulfill my love and dream, but needing additional income provoked me to become more serious about being a business owner. I figured out a system to increase my demand. As long as there is a demand for what you are offering, you also can generate income in your business. But without passion, you may give up on the dream too soon. Whatever concept you decide to birth, ask yourself am I creating my business to serve others and fulfill my passion? Can I generate enough money in my business to sustain my lifestyle and meet my clients' needs? Your business need both passion and profit to succeed. It cannot succeed with one and not the other. You need both.

I was recently speaking with one of my clients who has an idea to create an amazing invention, but before she can execute her idea, due to a lack of funds, she has to work in a field that she's not passionate about but what's profitable at the moment. Sometimes you have to choose profit over passion in order to do the very thing that you're passionate about at a later time. Oftentimes, you have to choose money or work in a field that pays the bills; and, it will generate the funds for the idea or desire that you're passionate about. Your job or career has just become your first investor.

To be successful in your business, allow your purpose, passion, and profit to work together. You may even have to start with another business idea that is more profitable than the one you're more passionate about to generate the income you need to launch the business you truly desire.

Many times, people get purpose and passion confused. In my definition, purpose in business is providing a product or service with an end goal in mind. It is when you aim to satisfy your clients and your goal is to generate profit. On the other hand, passion in business will cause you to provide a product or service to your clients without a target goal in mind—you are aimlessly offering a service but not making a profit. When you are passionate about something, oftentimes, it is a challenge for business owners to charge what the product or service is worth. We struggle with putting a dollar sign on passion. However, when you are in business, profit has to override passion, and you have to attract the right client who will pay for what you have to offer. Passion helps to define your business, and without profit, you will become discouraged, disgruntled, and dissatisfied with your results as a businessperson. Profit in a business helps to solidify your purpose for starting your business.

Perhaps, you started a business based on your passion, which is the hardest process. At least you have gotten started and accomplished what many wish they could do. But if you're going to stick with the business, now it's time to evaluate it and figure out how you can make your passion more marketable to help produce more income to help create longevity in your industry. Passion will drive you into the market, but profit will sustain you. Find the missing element in your industry and turn your passion into profit.

Mistake #2 -Not Investing In Yourself

I decided to poll a group of ten entrepreneurs and business owners who have currently been in business five years or more. I asked, "If you could go back and change anything about the way you do business, what would it be?" Surprisingly each one of them referred to the fact that they would invest in themselves by hiring a coach, a mentor, or accountability partner. And to become more educated in the behind the scene works of a business such as management and finances.

Before we realized the importance of investing in our success, things start falling apart. Honestly, I didn't realize the importance of investing in myself early on in business. I had a great idea and that's all I needed, so I thought. Epic failure mentality! The individuals who are most successful continue to invest in their mind, educate themselves or pay someone for their expertise. I closed the doors to Prints & Designs 4 Less because I didn't understand what it took to take my business to the next level.

As a tax professional, the IRS requires us to receive continuous education every year to stay abreast of the new laws and regulations in our field, which is one of the reasons, our company, Accurate Tax Service LLC, ranks in the top 10 tax firms since 2012 in our service areas. We are living in an era where everything is constantly changing and progressing; therefore, we have to stay edgy to our market. People are attracted to businesses that are relevant; and, the only way to stay attractive to your clients is to keep up with the trends, provide top-notch service to your clients, and stay knowledgeable about your industry.

One huge shift happened for me in business is realizing the need for a coach and why I needed the support and help from someone to build my business. After I decided to take a leap of faith and hire a coach, it changed the dynamics of my business. If I can be honest with you, you can do certain things yourself; however, you can avoid the frustration if you hire a coach in the startup phase of your business by allowing the experience and expertise of someone to guide you through the phase we all face when starting a business: setback. Imagine having an issue with your business and having that go-to person who is vested in your success, who isn't envious of you, who offers sound advice and his/her success is predicated on your success? That's what a coach can do for you.

There are people who know the answer to the problems you're trying to solve. And the right coach can provide you with shortcuts and methods to achieving your goals, but you have to find the type of coach that fits you. Let me help you understand what a coach can do for you and your business.

You may be asking, "What is a coach?" A coach like a GPS. You start out by inputting your starting point and your destination in the GPS, then it gives you different choices on how to arrive at your last stop. It gives you the option to take the long route, avoid interstates, back roads, accidents and traffic disturbance. A GPS will also give you the option to travel the long or the short distance.

A coach is the GPS of your business.

Coaches offer:

- Direction. Different routes and suggested ways to reaching your destination. Quite frankly, they offer you the short and safety route. If you could arrive quickly to your destination, why not equip yourself with the tools to get there faster?

- Advice. Suggested ways to bypass unnecessary mistakes and jump the long line of new owners who are stuck and struggling in their business.

- Guidance. A GPS knows what's ahead. Your coach sees farther than you can at this moment. He/she guides you down the right path according to your business goals. You trust them blindly as they hold your hand to assist you with arriving at your destination ahead of schedule and intact.

I ran my business for many years based upon the knowledge that I obtained through trials and tribulations, research, education, and by watching others; and that wasn't enough to help me, but I didn't know it. At the time, I was doing what I thought was right. I felt I could research everything on my own. I would join free webinars online and watch YouTube videos, which is okay, but at the end, I struggled with implementation and knowing what really applied to the right-now situation in my business. The information that you read, research or watch online can be good, but is it good for you at the moment. Free information rarely tells you the key points that you need for your business or how to implement what you learned. Now you're back at square one: frustrated. And still while getting information from everywhere, you find yourself like I would like to describe as a church hopper. Going from one church to another that's sending you backward instead of forward. It is as if you have everyone in your ear. Have you ever had what seemed like the whole world offering their opinion, but nothing is working out for you? That can be confusing.

When I became frustrated and business slowly started to decline, there was nowhere to turn. I was confused, frustrated, and broke and that's when I decided to start networking and find the coach who was best for me. After I found my coach, I disconnected from all the other voices that were offering opinions and soaked up everything my coach had to offer.

As a new business owner, you don't have to wait until your business fails, declines, or doesn't succeed before hiring a coach or invest in yourself. Why wait until you're about to shut down your business when someone is waiting to relieve your stress?

Currently, the market is saturated with amazing coaches. Find the one that is helpful for you and your business. You can find a coach for just about any type of situation or business, whether it's a life coach, sports coach, singing coach, or business coach. Some people work with more than one coach depending on the person's personal or business needs, but starting out in business, I suggest working with a business coach until you have applied everything you've learned from that person.

I wish I would have hired a business coach before I started my business, but at the time, I felt as if I couldn't afford one. The reality is my business couldn't afford not to have one. I know you've heard the saying, "If I knew what I know now back then, things would be totally different." Well, that's how I feel as I am writing this to you. If I knew how important it was to hire a coach in the startup phase of business, I honestly believe my business would be farther along than it is now. It may not make sense today to literally pay someone for their time, knowledge, and expertise, but it will help kick-start your business in the right direction.

Hiring a coach provides several benefits:

1. A coach stretches your thinking. Before I started my business, The Startup Business Factory, I was only interested in helping those in my community. I was thinking about the people who were connected to me on

social media, but my coach allowed me to see the possibilities outside of the people within my reach. She showed me how to grow my business. She showed me that what seemed impossible can be possible.

2. A coach helps bring clarity to your vision. If you find yourself stuck and if you're not generating enough funds to generate profit, before you quit, hire a coach. When you create a business, you know exactly what you want to do, but you may not know how to bring it from idea to execution. A coach will help you uncover missing elements in your business while helping you to think about every angle of your trade. Your coach helps bring clarity to those questions you will have when operating a business and answer questions that may be stagnating the growth of your business. You may know what to do, but struggle with how to do it. For example, you may know how to do hair, but struggle with how to attract your clients. Your coach will help with the "how".

3. A coach will help you see additional tunnels to increase your business revenue. Maybe you're generating funds, but not enough to take it to the next level. That's what a business coach is for: to help you create other streams of income for your business. Your coach will evaluate the products and services you're currently offering and

help you see added ways to generate income in your business.
4. A coach offers solutions. If you're struggling in your business, there's a solution, and it may or may not be found online. However, the suggestions found online may not apply to your business. You need someone who is experienced to help you answer those frustrating questions pertaining to you and your business. Why spend weeks researching answers or feeling like a failure when there's a solution—a business coach?

Many times a coach and mentor can be mistaken as providing the same service although they both use the same skills and approach at times. There are several types of coaches, and you may select one based on your needs, the coach's professional experience, and/or their promise to you after working with them. Business coaches provide training and instruction like a sports coach provide to his sports team for a short duration of time. A coach is more focused on solving a particular issue and looks for an immediate goal, solution, and achievement from the person being coached. Mentors provide support, offer wise advice and normally support you for a longer period of time than a coach. Mentors tend to be more focused on relationship building and development for a longer period of time. As a business owner, you may need both a coach and a mentor and sometimes a coach can provide both.

In order to grow, you have to challenge yourself to grow and from my personal experience, coaches and mentors help you to do that in business. Coach with those who have become an expert in the areas in which you are weak, who intimidate you enough to make you want to model after them. That's how I challenge myself to grow by surrounding myself with people who make more money than I do, who are wise in business, age, and experiences, and who benefits me more than I can benefit them. Push yourself in the areas where you are strong to sharpen your skills even the more so; and the areas you are weak, strengthen. Never become so boastful and proud that you can't be taught. Continue to grow and expand as a business owner. Your business will only grow as you are willing to grow. Find a coach or a mentor today.

The best way to find a coach is through social media, word of mouth and/or blogs. You may decide to have someone coach you who may not recognize themselves as a coach or have a certain level of education. You may choose them simply because you've watched them climb the ladder of success.

What do you look for in a coach?

1. **Determine your need for a business coach.** In what areas do you need a coach? Is it leadership training? Sales? Marketing? Define your goals. Determine your strengths and weaknesses. Decide which set, strengths or

weaknesses, you need to improve immediately that will help your business increase revenue the quickest.

Find a coach who can help you in that area.

2. **Determine what experience you require your business coach to have.** Do you want to work with someone who has been in business a certain amount of years? Someone who has generated a certain amount of business profit? Has proven results? Is a type A personality? What are your requirements? And don't be afraid to ask them how they can help you and by working with them, what is their promise to you.

3. **Determine your method of coaching.** Does your coach need to live in the same city? Do you want to be coached face-to-face? Online? I actually have two coaches: Aprille Frank-Hunts, Master Business Coach and President of Coach, Speak & Serve, provides coaching sessions through online methods and Felicia Phillips, Business Strategist, provides face-to-face coaching. Whatever your needs are, there is someone who can meet them.

Figure out a way to constantly invest in yourself by making it a part of your monthly expense. I can almost guarantee you that you will see a shift in you and your business.

Mistake #3 - Running Your Business as a Hobby

Money, money, money; we hate to say that we are in business to make money, but we truly are. We just haven't gotten bold enough to say it. Your priority may be to help and serve others, leave a legacy for your kids, or to be your own boss. Whatever the reason is, honestly speaking, you need money to achieve those goals. Therefore establishing a budget and having financial goals has to be a significant factor in your business. Initially starting out in business, finances may not be a top priority. That's why some business owners struggle with setting prices, paying themselves or lack paying monthly expenses. Oftentimes, we start because it's our passion, a hobby or an unfortunate or unforeseen circumstance that led us into business for ourselves, so we conduct our activity without an intent to generate a profit. After experiencing some level of frustration, that's when we decide to become more serious about our craft, then soon realize that we need money to do the things that we love to do in a more excellent and bigger way. When this happens, that's when we start shifting and changing the way we do business.

Recently, I was speaking with a young lady who is very passionate about her idea to provide a unique service to entrepreneurs. However, her passion causes her to struggle with charging for her services. After hearing that she was afraid to ask for what she felt her service was worth, my question to her was whether or not she intends to have a successful business. As much as we love what we do, we are more of a benefit to our clients when they are satisfied, and we are getting paid for what we do. Eventually, without funds, our business is negatively affected; and it's impossible to provide outstanding customer service day after day when our needs aren't being met. And your business can not survive very long without profit.

Without the right mindset, you cannot build a business successfully. A person who is involved in a hobby doesn't think like an individual who is a business owner. Priorities and focus areas are never the same.

The IRS breaks it down in a simple explanation to help you determine whether an activity is a business or hobby. According to the Internal Revenue Service, if you are engaged in an activity with no intent to make a profit, the activity you are engaged in is considered a hobby. A hobby can generate income and have expenses, which are filed on Schedule A of your tax return. If you are running a business, your income and expenses can be filed on Schedule C of your personal tax return if you are a sole proprietor or a LLC. It is truly all about the intent when it comes down to helping you determine whether or not your activities are considered a hobby or a business.

Money can change the way the government classifies your business. There are two terms that are relevant to help you codify the funding structure in your business: profit and revenue.

- Revenue is the amount of money your company brings in which can be broken down on a daily, weekly, monthly or annual basis. For instance, if you charge $19.99 for a product, then your company has generated $19.99 in revenue.

- Profit is income that exceeds the business expenses and payroll. The easiest way to determine your profit is to add all the business revenue generated for one month, subtract all your business expenses, including purchases for product and payroll for the month, and what's left over is your profit.

If a business doesn't generate profit three out of five years, it is considered a hobby. This will give you a better view as to whether or not the IRS has the probability to change your classification from a business to a hobby.

Take a moment to re-evaluate why you're in business. If you determine that you are in business to generate profit, then you have to run your business as a business —meaning you have to put structure in your business such as: set prices, establish policies, procedures, and operate with an intent to generate profit. As your business grows, you will discover how important it is to never compromise your business integrity, stop being afraid to charge your business worth, and feeling obligated to provide a discount to everyone who asks.

After coaching many business owners, the most important component is missing: a solid foundation. You may be one of many business owners who started your business without establishing it the legal way, meaning you came up with a business name and you started working it without knowing what's required of you. Have you applied for an employee identification number, filled out a sales and occupational tax application, if necessary, or established a separate business account—basically paid your dues for being a business owner? Now what components are missing from your business? Research what is required for city, county, and state laws for business owners in your area. Also, as a business owner, although it is not a requirement, you need systems in place when operating business in this day and age. For instance, if you are selling a product, do you have Square or some other payment processing account? Do you have a social space to connect with your customers such as Facebook business page?

If you want to take your business higher, you have to make sure that every *i* is dotted, and every *t* is crossed. You must operate on the integrity rule in business, which simply means that if you do right, money will come to you and you can avoid many roadblocks. Recently, I found out that I was out of compliance with the city of Birmingham. It was a mishap; however, I had a choice that day as I was speaking with the representative to lie to save over a thousand bucks or tell the truth. As a business owner, you will always be placed in compromising situations; however, I am more than confident that I made the right decision to operate in integrity. Make good choices as the CEO of your company, so you will never have to worry about others exposing your truth. Choosing to do what's right at the moment may cost you more, but it will save your business name and your reputation as a business owner in the long run.

According to the Internal Revenue Service Code Section 183, the following factors may help you determine whether your activity is for profit or a hobby:

1. **Does the time and effort put into the activity indicate an intention to make a profit?** Breakdown: How much time are you spending working on and in your business? For your business to grow, you have to spend time working it. I try to convey to others that you will spend more time running your business, especially in the startup stage, than you've ever spent working for anyone. You must make time for your business if you want it to grow and prosper. If you are a parallelpreneur—working a full-time job while running your business—you have to schedule the time to work your business during the hours that's most convenient for you and stick with it.

As a suggestion, here is a sample daily schedule for a parallelpreneur that works 9-5 p.m.

6:00 a.m. – 6:30 a.m.	Wake Up & Devotion
6:30 a.m. - 8:15 am	Exercise; Eat Breakfast; Get ready for work; Family duties
8:15 a.m. - 9:00 a.m.	Travel time to work
9:00 a.m. - 5:00 p.m.	Time devoted to your job
5:00 a.m. - 10:00 p.m.	Time devoted to your family
10:00 a.m. - 2 a.m.	Time devoted to your business

As a rule of thumb, you should be doing something in your business every day—whether it's networking and making the right connections, marketing, posting on social media, writing a blog, or just visualizing and dreaming about your next move. Is it easy to fulfill this task? Absolutely not, especially if you wear several hats; but it is necessary. You've heard the old saying that we make time for what we want. Being an entrepreneur means that you are responsible for making sure that your business goals are executed according to your vision even if you delegate the task. Ultimately, the rise or fall of your company rest in your hands; therefore, make no allowances for excuses.

Excuses are the enemy to productivity. We have too many excuses as to why we aren't making things happen in our business. That's why everyone isn't meant to be a business owner. The desire, drive, and determination isn't placed in everyone to do what you've been called to do. You were chosen to be an entrepreneur and since you've responded to the call, please realize that you have something unique and necessary to offer. The world is waiting for you. What would the world have been without the lightbulb or the invention of the computer? Now ask yourself, "What would the world be like without my business?" You cannot continue to put your business on the backburner. Otherwise, someone may be waiting to pick up where you left off.

My husband and I had an opportunity to purchase a rental house on the east side of town. It was an amazing deal that was move-in ready. Plus, it had $40,000 in equity. I convinced him not to purchase it, because I had allowed my fears to get in the way of our dreams. Of course, there were several other real estate investors waiting for us to renege on the purchase of the property. Since then, the house has been rented consistently for over the last seven years. We missed our window of opportunity. How many times have you said that you had a thought or that you have a concept, then you find out someone else is doing it? Well, it happens when your excuses and fears become the reason you hand your dream over to someone else.

Excuses will be the number one reason you don't put the time into your business. If this is what you truly long to do, you must not allow fear, time, or money to stop you from pursuing your goals. How can you eliminate the distractions in your life to find more time to work on your business?

2. **Do you depend on income from the activity?** Breakdown: Does your life depend on you making money from your business? Are you at the point of desperation that if this doesn't work out, you don't have anything else to rely on? If you depend on your business to supplement your income or if it is your main source of earnings, then the IRS understands you are more likely to work extremely hard to generate cash flow. Desperation breeds success. I never met a person who's been desperate to succeed and didn't.

Most people don't depend on money generated through a hobby. My life depends on our businesses being successful, because neither my husband nor I have a nine-to-five to rely on. All I have is the vision and dream that's is divinely inspired, and every decision I make leads me one step closer to it. I'm in pursuit of it. I'm focused. I'm driven. I'm determined to make it happen. Is this all you have? If it is, revisit your plan and methods of doing business and build towards the success you desire. Even if you are working a regular job, if you depend on your business income to pay for a specific bill or expense, the same efforts that full-time entrepreneurs put into their business, your determination should match.

If your goal is to have financial freedom through your business and you aren't making any money at this time, two things will happen: You will give up, or you will find a way to make it work. If your business is struggling, be honest with yourself and ask some very tough questions. Are you really doing everything you know to do to make it work? If you are, then it's time to seek outside help. Network. Revise your marketing plan. Get crystal clear on who you are servicing. Hire a coach or a mentor. If your business is going to thrive, you must change and implement. Don't be afraid to do things in a different way in order to get a better result.

3. **If there are losses, are they due to circumstances beyond your control, or did they occur in the start-up phase of the business?** Breakdown: Every business is expected to have a loss in the startup phase, but as time progresses, you should see that number reduce tremendously. As a taxpayer, your expenses must be ordinary and necessary for conducting your business. Remember, you really only have three years out of five to generate a loss before your business could possibly be classified as a hobby.

As a recommended tax preparer by the IRS, I see many times that business owners' expenses exceed their income because they aren't figuring out ways to increase their revenue. For instance, if you've been in business for three years and you have had the same loss year after year, something is wrong with that picture. A business owner who is serious about generating profits evaluates his business on a daily, weekly, monthly, and yearly basis and will not position the business to continue to operate on the same scale without making changes, corrections, or improvements. If you are experiencing financial loss in your business, why? And if you know why, then why haven't you done anything to change it? You need a plan to increase your revenue year after year.

Everyone have heard the saying that if we continue to do the same thing over and over again, but expect a different result that is the definition of insanity. For instance, my friend, Tae Lee, owner of First Alert Tax in Alabama and Georgia, placed tax signs out in the community her first year in business. After measuring her results, she realized that it would not benefit the company to use that same method of advertising the following year, since she didn't get the results she desired. This is an example of making the necessary changes instead of continuing to put money towards an area that would cause the business to have a loss.

4. **Do you have the knowledge needed to carry on the activity as a successful business?** Breakdown: What is your background? What experience do you have? We tend to think since we are good at doing certain things, we have the knowledge to run a business, which isn't always true.

There isn't one person who starts a business and knows everything about the industry they choose or have the knowledge to carry out the plan successfully. When my husband and I started our first graphic and printing company, we didn't know there were requirements as a business owner at the time; and although we succeeded in obtaining clients, we incurred many mistakes and lost several business opportunities, which eventually lead us to closing the doors to Prints & Designs 4 Less.

You can be good at producing products or have excellent service, but you may need someone to assist you with operating and managing your business. In addition, it is also my belief that every business owner should continuously seek education and training to obtain the proper knowledge to build a company successfully.

Also, you must consider and ask yourself a very hard question, whether you're meant to be a CEO or a leader in an establishment. You may have the skillset. You may be able to perform a job or service better than anyone; however, that doesn't mean you're meant to be a business owner. I found a quiz written by author and entrepreneur Carol Roth entitled, "Do You Have What It Takes to Be an Entrepreneur?" Out of the five questions, she asked, there was one particular question that stood out the most, "Are you a Santa or an elf?" Here's her quote found on Entrepreneur.com.

Are you Santa or an elf? Entrepreneurship requires managing a wide variety of tasks as part of the business, from marketing and accounting to training, customer service, and more. Can you wear multiple hats, as Santa does with Christmas, or do you prefer to be the elf that loves to execute specific tasks? Do you take initiative or do you want clear instructions? Santa make better entrepreneurs than elves do.

After reading the article, I realized that it's important to know your strengths and weaknesses to help you determine if you are a Santa or an elf. Being smart or good at making products or providing a service doesn't mean that you have what it takes to build a business successfully. You have to be honest with yourself and determine whether you are meant to travel the road to entrepreneurship. There are several things you should consider during your self-examination process:

- Do you have the resilience to withstand the hurdles and disappointments as a business owner?

- Should you support someone who's in the same industry as you desire to be in even if for a short period of time?

- Is partnership better for you in order to share the business responsibilities and decision-making duties?

- Should you contract your services?

There's a possibilities that you aren't meant to be the first in command, although, you may exhibit great qualities of a CEO.

And that's okay. Both leaders and CEOs serve very important roles in a business and both are necessary. Many find it hard to differentiate the two roles, which gives leaders the impression that they would make the perfect CEO. In short, according to Stever Robbins, Inc., a CEO is responsible for:

- Delegation
- Setting strategy and direction
- Modeling and setting the company's culture
- Building and leading the senior executive team
- Allocating capital to the company's priorities.

Leaders make sure that the CEOs' responsibilities are carried out. Many of the tasks that CEOs delegate are given to leaders in the company, who is responsible for a large percentage of a company's success or failure. CEOs can build a company from scratch, but a leader only has the potential to carry out what's been built. Sometimes leaders don't have the vision or patience to build a business from scratch, but once systems and strategies has been put in place, they can help move the company forward. So are you a CEO or a leader?

After an honest evaluation and if you agree this is where you belong, in the role of a CEO, then you need to obtain the knowledge, training, and coaching to build a thriving business.

You may have understood just enough to get started in your industry, but what you continue to feed yourself will help you overcome hurdles and obstacles you will face in your business.

5. **Have you changed your methods of operation to improve profitability?** Breakdown: Have you done everything you can to generate profit? What changes have you made? Have you increased your marketing? Have you determined your target market? Have you measured your results? If you desire to run a successful business, keep your goals in mind, but change your methods if you have to—or change your goals in order to keep the methods. Something has to change if you aren't generating profit or able to pay yourself. We've all heard it before that if we continue to do the same things over and over again and keep getting the same results that is the definition of insanity. You cannot continue to run your business the same way and expect to improve profitability. A business must always show signs of progression even when generating profits. You have to continue to stay relevant as a business owner. Your business has to constantly show signs of improvement. If you are improving profitability year after year, you have to continue being a forward thinker and keep up with the progressing market and the progressive behaviors of your clients. Clients will be satisfied with your service today, but ready to leave for the next business that draws their attention if you aren't staying relevant to the market. Large competitors should see you as a threat. As a business

owner, you will always have others gunning for your position. But establish the company that others seeks out.

My husband and I knew we had impeded the success of one of our competitors when two major chains proposed to purchase our company from us. We knew we were making an impact. Make your competitors know you. You aren't making an impact until you have the attention of your competitors.

Now after reviewing some of the requirements that the IRS uses to determine whether your activity is a business or a hobby, it's time to reevaluate your business model. What changes do you need to make? Create a written plan. Set goal dates. Make corrections. Fix what's broken. When you shift your mentality from worker to a CEO, you will find your business starting to change. Shift.

Mistake #4 - No Proof. No Trail.

Remember when people used to swipe their debit card at a cash register or write a check, then hold up the line writing that transaction in their checkbook register? Well, not anymore. Most of us feel as if we have a photographic memory. For instance, I recall this one time, I deposited fifty dollars in my account, then I pumped ten dollars in gas, use five dollars for my lunch and three dollars on my favorite drink from a local restaurant—it's amazing that I knew exactly how much was left in my account. And some of us are running our business the exact same way. We try to memorize everything until we forget that one transaction that can potentially throw our account into a negative. Memorization and checking your account every day may be helpful for you, however, according to the IRS, that is not considered having physical proof of funds spent that are ordinary and necessary business expenses.

The problem is that we tend to run our business the same way we run our personal life. As a recommended tax preparer by the IRS, year after year, I handle tax returns of business owners I know personally who run a business, but they don't have a paper trail, meaning they don't have proof of the income and expenses generated from their business. Then they have to spend additional money and countless hours reconstructing their business income and expenses, and they end up paying more in taxes because they can't deduct what they can't track.

As a business owner, you have to prove your income and expenses. Where is your paper trail? Where are your business receipts and/or documentation to back up what you claim on your tax return? How do you keep track of your income and expenses? You can't run a successful business without having a paper trail. Tracking your income and expenses gives you a clear view of your business. You can project the upcoming year, use it as a method to cut back on unnecessary expenses. You will be surprised how much money you may be spending unnecessarily when you track your outgo and compare it to your income. Creating a tracking system allows you to monitor what areas you can increase your prices or lower them. Many times business owners want to guess or use a rough estimate on their tax return, but the Internal Revenue Service doesn't care about what you put on your tax return. They are more concerned about what you can prove— paper trail—during an audit.

If I were to ask you how much your business earned last month, you should be able to go to your records to prove it. Now don't get me wrong, I am not saying you have to track it with a physical sheet of paper. There are many free systems you can use to track your income and expenses, but you must be willing to do the work. I recommend, a free app found in the App store or Playstore, Tax Pocket that allows individuals to track mileage, take pictures of receipts and other expenses and send it to your tax preparer or accountant at the end of the tax year. You may choose to hire someone to do the work for you.

From time to time, you may have to delegate the least important duties to you so you can spend more time on the things that are important in your business. Why spend countless hours running errands, cleaning the house, folding laundry, tracking receipts and other boring task, when that time can be spent with family, friends or working in your business. You may be like I was when we started out in business, broke and overwhelmed and unable to afford the additional services.

If you can't afford to hire someone, find a way to simplify your responsibilities or find someone who will trade services with you—barter. If you are going to manage that portion of your business, allocate time to track your business revenue and expenses. If your business is ever audited, using the excuse that you didn't have enough time to create a paper trail or to track your business activity won't keep you from being fined or penalized. Therefore, think about ways to create a paper trail in your business that is user-friendly for you and others to follow.

A paper trail is simply creating physical evidence of your business activity in written or electronic format. Implement systems and procedures during the startup phase of your business to make this process easier to adapt too as your business grows. If you have already started discarding receipts or important business documents, start today making the necessary adjustments to track everything going forward. When time permits, go back as far as you can to reconstruct any other proof of business activity.

It is my recommendation to create a filing system for receipts, invoices, applications, and other documents. It can be kept online through Google Drive, OneDrive or Dropbox. You can categorize your folders according to expenses, contracts, applications, and/or invoices as a suggestion. A paper trail is more than proving business income and expenses. There may be times you need more than financial records to use as proof of your business activity. You may need other documents such as invoices that you send to clients or applications that employees or contractors complete. Therefore, make it a habit keeping and filing anything related to your business.

Next, schedule time in the week to go through your receipts, enter in your mileage and manage the necessary part of your business that requires a paper trail. Recently, I discovered that someone that I know is undergoing an audit review from the IRS, and she was penalized a heap of money because she didn't have the right documentation in her files according to her business type. I suggest speaking with a tax preparer, bookkeeper, or accountant to educate yourself on what is considered necessary and ordinary business expenses and what information you need to track. Avoid the mistake of not having the right documentation for your business.

If you are going to be successful at establishing a paper trail, time management is going to carry a huge weight in getting this task completed without becoming overwhelmed. As a matter of fact, time management is the key to managing your business, family, career, money, and all the other aspect of your life. I suggest:

1. Scheduling an appointment on your calendar to keep track of everything you have to do, including returning phone calls and answering text messages and replies on social media. Schedule daily appointments to manage your life, and stick to the time. If you place it on your calendar that you are going to call a client back at 3:30, set an end time as well— block off 3:30 to 3:45 p.m. for that task. At 3:45 p.m., you should be hanging up the phone and moving on to the next appointment on your calendar. This will require that you stay focus and committed to the schedule. Also, add a few minutes between appointments to account for those that run over their allotted time or to give yourself a much needed break.

2. Create a daily to-do list. Hold yourself accountable to getting everything done on the list. There are times where you may have to put things on the next day's to do list, but don't make it a habit of putting things off.

3. Limit your time on social media. You can easily spend thirty minutes to an hour on social media when you could have been using that time for your business.

When you are on social media, make your time purposeful. There are times when I am scrolling on social media as entertainment or to keep up with family and friends that aren't purposeful, but when I'm on it during my business hours, I am on there with intentions to connect with clients, make my daily post, and/or respond to comments—in other words, I'm being intentional about my time.

4. Give yourself twenty-four hours to get the task done. If you're like me, you are probably managing and juggling several projects at one time. It can be hard to decipher which project is most important, so a one week project can easily turn into a three-month project if you aren't careful with your time. Additionally, it may appear as if you're not accomplishing any of your tasks or goals in a timely manner. This may lead to procrastination or to you giving up. As a suggestion, take one of your projects and give yourself twenty-four hours to get it done. No excuses. Remove all the distractions, and for the next twenty-four hours give it all you have. You will be surprised at the amount of work you can get done in that short period of time.

5. Schedule 90-minute work sessions. Recently, my business coach, Aprille, challenged us to shut out the outside world

and work in our business for 90 consecutive minutes. That was the best exercise I have ever done in my life. I was amazed at how much work I was able to get done during that time. I suggest trying this method several times throughout the day.

We all have complained about not having enough time in a day to get our work done, however, if you try one of the methods mentioned above or just make up in your mind that you are going to become more focused on your goals, you will be surprised at how much work can get done when you are deliberate with your time.

Again, create systems that will help you manage and organization your income, expenses, invoices, etc., more effectively in your business. The more organized and structured you are, the easier it will be to create a paper trail.

Mistake #5 - Mixing Business & Personal Funds

If you are using your business funds for transactions not related to your business, stop! What you have just described is comingling funds: using business income as personal money. Several ways that you may be doing this is putting gas in your car using your business account when the travel isn't related to business, paying your personal bills from your business account, taking your friends out to eat and claiming it as a business expense, just to name a few. I discovered many times new business owners assume that if they put in the effort and time to generate the income, then it is considered "their money." This is another reason why it's important to understand what it takes to run a business successfully.

Other examples of comingling money between personal and business usage is:

- **Depositing business funds into your personal account**. If a check is made payable to you, and it was for a service you provided, whether the check is deposited into your business account or your personal account, the funds are still considered business income. The issue is depositing the money into your personal account and forgetting to categorize it as business income. This is one of the many reasons business funds should be deposited into a business account. When funds are deposited into a business account, it is easily trackable and can be used as proof of income when applying for business credit, trade lines, or even personal loans.

- **Making withdrawals for personal use without documentation.** When you withdraw money from your business account, be sure to keep track of receipts and have proper documentation such as invoices, profit and loss statements, bank reconciliation statements, etc., proving that the transactions are business related. If a business owner withdraws money without proper documentation, it becomes personal taxable income.

- **Using one account for both your personal and business usage**. Every business owner should have a business account. This helps with managing income and expenses more easily, and depending on the entity structure, and this can cause the business unnecessary penalties.

Like many business owners, if I were to take a poll today to ask if you have a business account, you would probably raise your hand. Now if I were to ask you to keep your hand raised if you use that business account solely for business purposes, almost everyone's hand would come down. As long as you are using the account for both ordinary and necessary business expenses in carrying on your business, it is considered for business purposes, according to the IRS.

Sometimes, there can be a fine line between business and personal income and expenses. For example, if you drive to a business meeting and put gas in your car, you have two options: claim the actual gas you paid for travel as a business write off or claim the number of miles on your tax return. If you decide to claim the gas expense, it is easy to track and verify if the transaction was made out of your business account.

It's vital not to mix your funds, especially if you are an LLC. An LLC protects your personal assets from your business assets. In a case of a lawsuit, if you lose a case against your business, your personal assets cannot be touched. However, you can forfeit that right by becoming liable for your business debt if you use your company funds as your personal income. Don't lose your protection. Separate your business from your personal funds today.

Also, I recommend establishing a business account at a bank that's different from your personal account. As long as you have easy access to the funds, and you are looking at the money every day, you will be tempted to use it to meet a need.
Move it to another bank—far, far away from temptation.

You may have started to mix your personal funds with your business income for several reasons: you may be struggling to generate revenue in your business, lack of knowledge, or what my parents would consider, just plain hardheaded. Are you ignoring the laws and rules to being a successful business owner? Don't! If you've started, stop! If you are serious about being a business owner, you cannot break laws, rules, and regulations. If you decide to ignore the laws, expect to reap it in your business. You can't expect others to be faithful to your business if you aren't faithful or if you can't obey. It's called reaping and sowing; and, it works in both our personal and business life. You can sow a bad seed in one area and reap it in unexpected places even in your business.

Did you know that the IRS requires you to obtain the knowledge to run a business? It doesn't mean you are required to have a business degree, but if you are ever audited, saying, "I didn't know" isn't a justifiable reason to avoid penalties. You should understand how to do everything in your business even if you don't like too.

How many times have you heard about famous basketball players or entertainers becoming bankrupt after learning that millions of dollars were stolen from their account(s)? Although you may pay someone to manage your books, every business owner should understand small business finances. Educate yourself and understand the dos and don'ts to running a successful business especially finances. Attend network mixers, business seminars, and different classes offered in your trade. Having a lack of knowledge is not excusable in a court of law. That's why learning the importance of managing your business funds and managing in integrity is paramount to your business success.

One of the main reasons that business owners mix both personal and business funds is due to a lack of money. The only way to resolve this issue is to generate more income. What can you do right now to generate funds for your business? For some of us, it may be partnering with others, joining a network marketing venture, or obtaining a second job. If your business is important to you, raise capital, ask for it, or sell used items.

There are times in business when you need to use your personal funds for business expenses. There are several ways to loan your business money, but a paper trail is going to clearly define the agreement. If you have to use your personal funds for your business, withdraw it from your personal account and deposit it into your business account, then make the business transaction. When the business is financially able to pay you back, have documentation of the withdrawal from your personal account and documentation showing the exact amount of money you withdrew from your personal account was deposited into your business account and reimburse yourself. Or become an investor for your company by drawing up a contract between you and your business since you are a separate entity, and charge interest for the loan.

After speaking with Tim Mbogo, entrepreneur, accountant, bookkeeper, founder of Kickin' Styles, and tax preparer, we both agree that you have to look at what you give or loan to your business as an investment. It's your beginning capital. You're not losing funds when you invest in your business. If you aren't willing to invest in your business, no one else will. In an attempt to borrow money for your business, loan officers are going to ask for financial records of the amount you have personally invested in the company. If you aren't willing to go the extra mile for your business, don't expect others including investors or loan officers too.

As a business owner, it is imperative that you forecast your financial goals to know exactly how much you need to make daily, weekly, monthly, quarterly, and annually to reach your goals. Your target goals should be based on real numbers. Don't pull a number out of the sky and say that you want to make $20,000 a year and your business isn't capable of producing that amount. Many times we set our financial goals too high when we haven't made the first dollar. We all want to generate six or seven figures in our business, but that's not real numbers for you if you haven't made your first thousand (profit) yet. Being a six figure business owner can happen, but it may not happen as quickly as you would like it too. If you are going to reach your financial goals, any successful business requires money and an achievable, actionable, step-by-step plan to achieve it. And it's okay to start small, but aim high.

If you are a startup business owner, you may be wondering how to acquire enough money to open a business if your funds are limited. There are several ways I suggest:

1. **Put yourself on a strict budget and save the old-fashioned way**. We all spend money unnecessarily. Making the choice to be good stewards over your finances will help save money for your business and your family. Eliminate all unnecessary pleasures—for now. Remember your goal.

2. **Withdraw money from your 401(k).** If you are under the age of 59.5, you will face a penalty for early retirement withdrawal. Are you willing to be penalized to fulfill the desires of your heart and do what you have always wanted to do? Imagine starting your business and creating more than enough income to replace the money you withdrew and more. As a tip, be sure to get federal taxes taken out so you will not be faced with double taxation at the end of the tax year.

3. **Join a network marketing business.** Network marketing businesses are one of the quickest roads to financial freedom. Everything you need to start the business is included in the fee startup package. You can quickly launch a network marketing business for less than three hundred dollars depending on the firm you join. Some of my favorite network marketing

businesses are: It Works, Mary Kay, Total Life Changes, and Paycation.

4. **Partner with another business owner.** Who can you go into business with who has the same or greater drive, determination and motivation as you? It's not about having your name in the spotlight. If it were up to me, people wouldn't have to know my name as long as I could generate the amount of money I desired behind the scenes. Partnering with someone who has the same desire and who can split the cost of startup is a plus.

5. **Host a yard sale.** What do you have in your closet or garage that you can sell? We hold on to many items in hopes of using them at a later time. Let it go so you can earn enough money to start the business of your dreams. If you build a profitable business, you can always buy at a later time what you sold.

6. **Get a second job.** Many of you may be currently employed, and your funds are directed towards your family and those things that are a necessity. If you find a part-time job, come up with a six- to twelve-month sacrificial plan to put your extra earnings in your business.

The aforementioned are suggested ways you can use to raise capital for your business. Start with a plan. Know exactly how much you will need to start your business, and figure out a way to generate those funds so you won't start off lacking integrity by comingling funds. Even if you haven't generated money in your business, you don't have to wait until you have money in order to put the right systems in place. Many reasons business owners become stress because they wait until funds are in place to put structure and systems in order. Your business can take off tomorrow, will you be ready or will you be stressed wishing you would have taken the time, while you had time, to implement structure?

Mistake #6 - No Plan. No Pay.

How many jobs have you worked and didn't receive pay? None, right? Well, why work for yourself without compensation? When you started your business, one of your goals should have been to supplement your income and to live a life of financial freedom. How did you lose sight of your financial goal? The best way to service others is for you to meet your financial goals which position you to meet the needs of others.

It's easy to become discouraged in the process, when you have not implemented a plan to pay yourself. Paying yourself is just as important as it is to pay your bills. This is one of the main reasons many business owners comingle funds, or they give up on their business entirely. Wouldn't you agree that you spend more hours working for yourself than you've ever spent working for a job, yet you pay yourself the least or you don't pay yourself at all? That's a problem, and it's one of the many reasons businesses fails. It is an epic disgrace to you if you are working without paying yourself. You shouldn't be surprised that many people like to brag about being a business owner, yet they are broke. It is imperative that you figure out how much you would like to make during the startup phase.

After you have determined how much you would like to pay yourself, here is a simple formula that will help you to quickly understand how you can achieve your goal easily.

Let's say you are offering a service and you want to make an additional thousand dollars a month from that one service. If you provide several services, decide how much you would like to generate from each service. On a sheet of paper, write $1,000. Next, make four columns and label them *Per Day, Per Week, Biweekly,* and *Monthly*. In this example, you are going to work five days a week. There are four weeks usually in a month, so for biweekly, your total is five hundred dollars (divide a thousand dollars by two). Divide one thousand dollars by four weeks, which equals $250 a week. Divide $250 by five days a week, which equals fifty dollars a day.

Your example should look similar to this:

I WANT TO EARN AN ADDITIONAL $1000 A MONTH WORKING ONLY 5 DAYS A WEEK, BELOW IS MY BREAKDOWN ON HOW TO ACHIEVE IT.			
PER DAY	**PER WEEK**	**BIWEEKLY**	**MONTHLY**
$50	$250	$500	$1000

All you need to make is fifty dollars a day to make an additional thousand dollars a month, which adds up to twelve thousand dollars a year. Now, what service or product can you sell five days a week to generate fifty dollars a day in profit? This formula is more than achievable, and once you reach your thousand-dollar goal, then raise it by another thousand and so forth. Before you know it, you will be bringing in an additional two and three thousand dollars a month.

One of the worst decisions you can ever make is starting out in business without a plan to pay yourself or not having a financial projection which includes your salary. Once you get into the habit of not paying yourself, it is hard to break it, but it can be done. So if you are reading this guide before you start your business, you are in the position to start out right. I know how it feels to see the money generated in your business, and just about all of it has to go towards sustaining the business, which can be frustrating. That's why it's important not to lose sight of your financial goals when you are putting all the pieces together to run a successful business. Once you lose sight of your financial goals, you may eventually lose integrity, hope, and sight of your dreams and evidently quit. It's hard doing what you love broke.

Whether we want to admit it or not, money answers all things—it is the answer to many of the issues we are facing today. Now, that statement doesn't mean money is the totality of your happiness, but it can have a great percentage to do with your well-being. Many of us are afraid to say we want to have financial freedom in our lives and that we created our businesses to obtain it. One of the reasons many of us end up not having financial freedom is because we have a hard time believing we can truly achieve it. Your upbringing has a lot to do with the way you handle your financial situation. If you have seen people struggle financially, then it's easy to think that's the norm. Therefore, you have to change the way you see money in order to obtain what you desire. Money is like any other thing we want. If we manage what we have well, then we have a better chance of improving our lives. If we don't manage it well, it will have the reverse effect on us. We are happy when we have money and when we are able to give to ourselves, family, friends, and to great causes. As Mark Twain would say, "The lack of money is the root of all evil."

Do you know how embarrassing, downcast, and horrible it feels to have a desire to help and give when you can't? I remember sitting in church, and my pastor would ask for a special offering, but I couldn't give it. My heart wanted to, but my pockets couldn't afford it. Pastor Willie B. O'Neal of Mt. Canaan Full Gospel Church, stopped in the middle of his sermon and said that God was going to make me a millionaire; and I would be able to give like I wanted to. It has been more than fifteen years since he spoke it into my life, and I am proud to say that I am the fulfillment of a prophecy. I am grateful to know that I can give because I've learned how to pay myself early on in business and followed biblical principles.

Paying yourself is an investment or reimbursement for all the things you have done and will do to build your business. Therefore, if you invest in your business, at some point the business has to pay you back. Don't go another day without figuring out a plan to pay yourself. There are several ways to do this as a business owner. However, 100% of what comes into the business is not considered payroll especially if you receive cash payments. If you charge $29 for a product, you can't keep $29. Barbers, Beautician, Lawn Service Technicians and others who accept cash payments on a daily basis, definitely need a payroll and expense system in place to keep from spending all the revenue that comes in at one time. You have to allocate every dollar that comes into your business. My suggested way is to create a payment system for yourself is based upon percentage.

Let's say you own a shoe store and you've purchased a 12case of shoes for the wholesale cost of $239 plus shipping of $40. The total amount for the case is $279 ($239+$40) or $23.25 ($279/12 shoes) per shoe. As a suggestion to see your initial investment of $23.25, at the minimum, the general rule is to markup the shoes by 100%, which is $46.50. Most business owners will round that amount to retail at $49.99. Sometimes you can't sell every pair; therefore, you have to markup the price of the shoes just enough that you don't lose money when you need to offer a sale or a discount before the change of season or for other reasons. Remember, $23.25 goes back into the account to reinvest in other shoes (that's the amount you paid per shoe). The balance is $26.74 ($49.99- $23.25). What percentage of that amount goes towards payroll, expenses, and business savings from every shoe? It has to be up to you, but your plan must include ways for you to feel happy and excited to work for a company that can afford to pay you.

Revisit and revise the plan to include your payroll. Do not compromise. You may have to increase your prices on your product or services. Add an additional stream of income. Reduce your overhead. But build a business that can provide financial freedom in the startup phase. Keep in mind all the things that you hoped your business could offer you and others when you're battling in your mind whether or not your business can afford to pay you. You can't afford another moment to continue to build your business without getting paid. Make the adjustment today.

Mistake #7 - Limiting Your Income Potential

When my husband, Michael, and I started our shoe store, Strictly Heels to service women between the ages of twenty-five and thirty-five who wore at least a four-inch, sexy, high heel shoe, we did well in the business. However, we were not making the amount of money we needed to pay our bills and most importantly to pay ourselves initially. We sold out of shoes through presales, and we were shipping shoes all over the world. In less than two months, we were totally debt free as a business and making a profit. However, we needed to figure out a way to generate more money for payroll and expenses while keeping prices competitive because of our target market.

I loved selling shoes, and I knew I was making a difference and an impact on women who purchased them, and most importantly, I was making women feel good about themselves. It's an indescribable feeling to wear a pair of heels that makes you feel sexy and wanted. That's why we loved to see the reaction we got from our clients on a daily basis.

Although there were several shoe stores, I knew we were offering unique items that were stylish and affordable. These were not your everyday work shoes; these were the shoes you wear on a date or a night on the town. I could spot a Strictly

Heels shoe from miles away, and since I only sold twelve pair, not many people had the shoes we were offering. After a while,

I realized I wasn't maximizing our income potential with only offering four-inch heels when clients would come and ask for additional products we weren't selling. It was like I was watching money walk right out the door. Now the question was how was I going to continue to do what I loved, service my customers, keep my prices affordable, and make more money? The answer was right in my face. I started listening to what my clients wanted and what they needed. I heard Lisa Nichols, one of the world's most-requested motivational speakers, say that your clients are the experts. They will tell you what the market needs, and it is our job as business owners to service them.

As a business owner, look for the underserved areas in your market by listening to your customers, and as a result, you will increase your business income, which is a win-win situation. If several clients are requesting a service or product, there is a demand. Solve a problem, generate more revenue for your business.

You will miss out on generating additional funds for your business if you do not listen to your clients' desires. People will tell you what they want or need. However, you cannot be caught up in trying to push your agenda as a business owner. The business was created to serve others for a cost. The definition of a business is to provide a good or service for others at a cost.

As a newbie in the shoe industry, I was set in my business mindset. I was only going to offer four-inch heels or higher, but when my clients stopped buying and shifted their business to my competitors, I had to figure out a way to remain relevant.

I answered one important question: Why was I losing out to my competitors?

Your business may have started on passion or a vision based on your wants and desires, but if you're going to stay in business, you have to turn it into a customer service-based business. My clients started asking for products that I didn't have and one day it clicked to offer additional items that could supplement our income. That's when we decided to offer wedges. Once we did this, our clientele grew, and so did our bank account. We had tons of clients who loved the idea of wearing high heels, but every woman loves options. Now we created a win-win situation for both our clients and us. We made adjustments to our plan, but we stayed true to our vision.

When you're on the hunt to grow your business, it's best to start with the ones who are already doing business with you. Ask them for their opinion. What would they like to see you offer? Be brave and ask. If I was stuck on only offering one product and if I had a one track mind in business (doing things my way), I would have missed the opportunity to grow our business. You have to stay one step ahead of your competitors and be known as the problem solver in your industry.

When I couldn't drive traffic to our social media pages or website, I solved the problem. I decided to host shoe shows. After the first shoe party, my team and I realized we still needed to add another product. Although we were attracting many clients, the profit is the determining factor of a successful business. We weren't making enough money. We still needed to add an additional product in order to service more clients, which equated to more money. That's when we added jewelry and accessories. Think about other items or services you can add to your brand. You can keep your main goal in mind; however, always offer choices.

When my husband and I established Kingdom Care Academy, we were offering childcare services, then we started offering after-school care. In our tax business, we were only offering tax preparation, then we started offering bookkeeping services, payroll, accounting and other financial packages. Every business should always have more than one source of income.

There are different ways you can generate additional revenue in your business by offering another service or product. You need to know how much you want to profit, then determine what services you can offer to help add income. It's okay to start with one product; however, listen to your clients, and ask questions to determine what's next, and before you know it, you will be creating unlimited income in your business. After reaching one level of success in your current business, you will find yourself dreaming and thinking bigger than where you are. Fulfillment gives birth to the desire to do more.

Mistake #8 - Prideful, Not Asking For Help

My personal tax return was prepared one time by a tax professional, Ms. Dumas in Westend, Alabama. I was fascinated by the way she would input information into the computer system and how versed she was when it came to explaining the tax laws. Being in her presence sparked an interest in me, and ever since then—more than sixteen years ago—I've never allowed anyone to prepare my taxes. The following tax season, I started preparing taxes for my family and friends, and throughout the years, I've continued to do so. I didn't become serious about being a tax professional until five years ago. After working for a tax company, my husband and I decided to launch Accurate Tax Financial Service, LLC. We took the vision and literally ran with it. Now, here's the problem: I was afraid to ask for help. I could have started in business years ago as a professional if I would have been bold enough to seek out the counsel of someone who has knowledge and a proven track record in my industry. Many times we delay our dreams because we are shamed and too embarrassed to ask for help. And most times, the assistance we desire come from the people least expected and they don't mind guiding us in the right direction.

Oftentimes, when you are in the presence of successful people it sparks a flame in us, however, it hinders us as well. We think because they have achieved a certain level of success that they look down on us since we are not where they are.

owever, it's our lack of confidence in ourselves that makes us feel that other people see us the same way we view ourselves. The right person will help you. They aren't intimidated by your growth or your potential to supersede them. However, we are intimidated by their success. We start overthinking. Getting in our head. Having conversations with ourselves about the way they "may" see us. When we create false illusions of how other people view us, we tend to block the help we need that is standing right in our face. That's pride.

At times, I took on full responsibilities and more than I could handle because I was prideful. Didn't know how to say no and I wasn't good at delegating. The Leo in me liked to be in control and be involved in every aspect concerning our business. Over time, I didn't realize I was allowing pride (trying to do everything on my own) to give birth to what could have been an epic failure. Pride comes before a haughty fall and I almost did because I wasn't servicing my clients the way I knew I could. I was easily frustrated and bothered. I was still missing important moments with my family, and I was exhausted. Some nights I wasn't getting but a few hours of sleep, then I'd repeat that cycle for months at a time. I knew how I wanted things to be, and I was the only one who knew how to get it done, so I thought. This is a great example of being a good leader, but a horrible manager. It was as if I couldn't trust other people with my vision. Plus, I loved the fact that when people asked who did this or that in our business that I could stick my chest out and say I did it, although, the pressure placed on me almost made me have a mental breakdown. Can you relate to the pride in my life? CEOs must learn to be good leaders and managers.

Maybe you are where I was, about to abort the vision before getting started out of frustration and feeling overwhelmed. Are you exhausted from your business because you're doing everything? Well, I have a solution: Ask for help. All you have to do is ask. I didn't realize that people were waiting to join my team and willing to use their resources to help me. In order to run a successful business, there is no way you can do it all. Yes, I understand that it takes money that you may not have and you can't afford to pay someone right now. There are a couple of things you can do, but first, you must be crystal clear and gain clarity on the type of person you need for your business. What skill set must they possess? If they are missing a skill set, can you train them or are they trainable? What exactly do you need this person to do? Get clear.

Connect with other business owners who offer the service(s) you lack and trade services. For instance, if you sell shoes and you need a banner made, you can ask a graphic designer to make your banner in exchange for free shoes.

The key to asking is to move past your fear and not be afraid to put yourself on the line, and be honest with where you are. Asking doesn't mean you're always going to get a yes. As a matter of fact, you will never get the answer you want all the time. You may even feel rejected by some, however, you have to keep trying until you find that one person who is ready to barter with you. Another tip is to solicit volunteers. One of my clients, Yogi Dada, is a well-known artist who creates wearable art. She solicits volunteers for her business all the time. In her language, they are considered interns. Many people know her by her amazing ear bangers. You can support her business by going to social media and searching Yogi Dada. After having a session with her, I suggested that she mentor other artists and as repayment, they would serve her business. Can I tell you how happy, relieved, and stress-free she has been since she received additional help for free? Plus, she is able to give back through mentorship. She needed help, the volunteers needed a mentor. Who wins? Everyone involved.

How can you do the same within your business?

My husband and I found a location and established everything—and I truly mean everything—while managing to take care of an infant and a son who was involved in every sport. And did I mention, I was working full-time during the day and my husband was leading The Celebration Church as the senior pastor? We were determined we were going to open the doors to Accurate Tax during the week at 4 P.M and on Saturdays at 10 A.M. My husband provided all of the customer support, and I prepared taxes while my son assisted with just about everything we told him to do. We created the logo; the mission statement; the vision statement; formed the business structure, including all the graphics and marketing; prepared the taxes; handled customer complaints; printed checks; and provided technical support. And people wonder why I don't like excuses.

We were limited on funds, and I immediately became a one-man show. Now, don't get me wrong, a one-man show means having the support from my husband and kids, but at times, I felt as if I was still creating a business and running it all by myself. When you have a vision, it doesn't matter who supports you. You will have a connection to the business that others may not. I'm sure, I work harder in Accurate Tax than my husband, and I'm more than positive that he works harder at The Celebration Church than I do. Although we support each other, whoever had the vision first will have more of a drive to see it succeed than those who back it. If Accurate Tax was to collapse, I'd feel as if I were having a breakdown, but my husband may not feel that way because our heart beats differently for it. So if you're a husband and wife team, it's okay if the supporting spouse doesn't give as much as you do. There's only one visionary, but shared responsibilities.

I was limiting my income potential by being a one-woman show, and that's when I realized I had to bring on additional teammates and sow my profit. The only way to get additional help in my business, bring exposure to the brand, and to reach my business financial goals was to bring on additional people and give them a percentage of my income—what I call sowing my profit.

I know you are saying, "Is this chic really serious about giving money away?" I understand if you don't have any money to give away, however, you can't limit your income potential because you are afraid to share the growth with others who have an interest in your same industry. Why not make them a part of your team? For a percentage of your profit, you can give them an opportunity to serve more people under your brand. With the number of potential new clients they bring in, you are making additional income because you can't reach their clients on your own. Even if you profit two dollars from their clients, that's two dollars more than what your business had. Let's say that you have a product to sell. If you add sales consultants to the team as independent contractors—they don't get paid until they sell a product—you can share with them a portion of the revenue generated.

Your process may not work exactly as the example that I described above, but if you want your business to grow, you can't do it alone. If you are the only person on your team, you are probably lacking structure, feeling overwhelmed, and you're unable to expand your business because you are stretched thin. The solution is to sow your profit. I'm at the point in my business that I'd rather take a risk hiring someone to be a part of my team than to limit my creativity with stress. As the boss or CEO of your company, you can't be tied into every aspect of the business. You have to keep your thoughts clear in order to think about ways to grow. Furthermore, you need someone who is willing to go in the trenches with you— someone whom you can bounce ideas off and who will basically help you. Two heads are always better than one.

You can find creative ways to get others involved in your business. Determine what you have to offer in lieu of their services and determine how they can help you and seal the deal. One of my friends, Keisa Sharpe, founder of All Shea Natural, is great with networking with other business owners. You can find her products in just about every small business storefront in her surrounding area. She realized she couldn't do it alone, and now she is becoming a household brand because of the visibility of her products through the help of others. Don't be a one-man business show your entire life.

Use the chart below to help you create your dream team.

In the first column, list all the positions within your company. In the second column, list who is currently filling the position. If you are, write your name. If no one leave blank. In the third column, list who you would like to fill the position. Find people who can fill these positions even if you aren't ready to hire them. In the fourth column, list what it would cost you to hire them. If you can't afford to bring them on your team, find a way to raise the money, create an additional stream of income, cut back on expenses, but set a goal to have them aboard your team by a certain date. Without the key people in position, it will continue to limit your income position.

Position	Who Currently Fills the Position?	Who Would You Like to Fill it?	Cost

Mistake # 9 - Separating You from Your Business

While waiting for a meeting to start, I saw a young lady from my peripheral vision with a huge smile walking towards me. I tried to avoid her by turning my head, but I could tell she was coming, and there was no stopping her. I braced myself for her comment and she said, "Hi. Don't you own the tax business with a bullseye as the logo?"

Now by this time, my guard was up, defenses were in place, and I had prepared myself for her complaint about my service, one of my teammates, my business, or something. Well, to my surprise, she gave rave reviews on our business and the strides we are taking to become a household name. She said that every time she sees a bullseye logo she thinks of Accurate Tax. We stood there talking about business as if we had known each other for a long time – all because she recognized our brand. Notice that she didn't walk up to me and say, "Are you Dee?" She identified me based upon our brand image. That speaks volumes.

As a business owner, as much as we would like to separate ourselves from our business, we can't, especially as a newbie in the industry. Initially, people are going to do business with you because they like you or they want to support you. Applause for those people, however, they are identified as supporters, and their support is probably limited unless you can transition them into clients. In the startup phase, you are going to need tons of supporters, but your goal should be to transform them into paying clients. Much of that has to do with your personal brand.

Who you are certainly is a reflection of your business. It's all about you. When I first started in business, you could see my family's pictures on just about every piece of marketing material. I made sure we were smiling, engaged with one another, and color coordinated. We wanted people to see us as a family business. If people saw us as a family business, then just maybe they'll invite their family to do business with us. We wanted to be appealing to our audience. All of it was part of our marketing strategy because if people can put a face with the business, they will feel more connected to us. And the more connected your clients' feel, the more money you will generate.

People are emotional buyers. I know this may sound manipulative, and you may not agree with my logic, but hear me out. You have to connect to the emotions of a person in order for them to spend money. Why do you think salespeople like talking with wives over husbands? Why do you think women are the best salespeople? Women understand the importance of an emotional connection and an emotional attraction. A person can be so emotionally connected to you that they will buy from you just because you're the one who's selling it. Just like some of you may have purchased this book, because of your support for me. I'm sure you have connected with other individuals because of an image, social media post, blog, webinar, conference calls, Periscope or Facebook live. All are ways to influence others and use as a way to connect with your clients. You matter in your business. Buyers are getting away from large corporation and prefer small business owners because of the connection they have with the person in position of power, you. People are logging on to Facebook live or liking your post because they are connected to you.

One day my husband and I decided we were going to purchase our first home together and we needed a realtor. We went through a website of realtors and chose a professional based upon a picture. I distinctly remember this one girl I wanted to choose, but I decided not to because her hair wasn't appealing to me. Yes, her hair was a turn-off. The moral of the story is that your image matters. It's about having the right image connected to your business, product, or service. Everyone doesn't have to like your style, but because you matter so much to your business, own whatever you decide. If you're comfortable wearing purple hair with big glasses like me, own it. Your appearance matters because you matter. Why do you think pastors post pictures of themselves and their church family? To entice others to be a part, to connect to others, and to give the prospect a peek of what it's like to be connected to his or her church. It's all a marketing strategy, and it's about putting a face to the service or product.

People want to do business with those who are kind, patient, and trustworthy and who have a good reputation, morals, and values. Will everyone like you? No, but let the good works that you do speak for you. Take a moment to think about the person you consider to be a con-artist, liar, mean, devious, or lack integrity. This person has every character flaw you can think of, yet, this same person decides to become a business owner and opens one of the hottest, most successful boutique in the city. Can you do business with this person knowing his or her lack of character? Probably not.

Again, you matter. What you exhibit and give off is important to your business. Negative characteristics don't disappear because you've decide to become a business owners. You can try to subdue them, but eventually, it will spurt over into the business if you don't put forth a conscience effort to change them. You must exhibit a stellar reputation, be trustworthy, likable, honest, and appeal to your target audience in your going to build a consistent flow of customers.

You are your business, and having a business name does not distinguish you from your business. Your business name helps identify the type of services or products you provide. One of the mistakes that many new business owners make is thinking their brand message, marketing, products, business, and services are separate from them. You are the message. You are your brand. You are your advertising. You are your marketing. You are your business. Everything you do, everything you say, and everything you post on social media must be intentionally. What you do in your personal life will affect your business — either negatively or positively.

As you build your brand, you must be aware that you must be personally fit for the scrutiny that comes with being a business owner. When you become a business owner, you become a public figure. Think about it. How many times do you refer people to your business page, but they always find a way to revert back to your personal page? They want to know you. They want to know your interest—what you like and don't like—and your beliefs. Your clients become interested in what you have to offer by becoming interested in you first. If you can't handle the pressure of being a public figure, then you will limit your success in business unless you choose to have someone else as the face of your message.

If you brand yourself properly, it will jumpstart your business for success. My favorite way to brand my businesses is to make myself visible to others at social and networking events. According to Adam Small, founder of the Strategic Business Network, "Networking is the single most powerful marketing tactic to accelerate and sustain success for any individual and organization." Networking is about being in the presence of the right people and helping others to know who you are outside of social media and email blasts. I've heard someone say that it's not about who you know, it's about who knows you.

Networking helps you build strong relationships. When people are comfortable with you, they become comfortable with your brand. Networking is more than just having an elevator speech and telling others about your brand, it's about helping others succeed in their respected field. When you can help others, they will find a way to help you. Once you gain the attention and influence of others, let them know in a bold, authentic way what you and your business stand for. You don't have to be pitchy or aggressive with your approach. Eventually, you will have an opportunity to discuss business. When you build the relationship, people will desire to know what you do and how they can support you even if they don't need your service.

Mistake #10 - Lack of Consistency

For six months, my husband brought me a gift once a month, and I loved that he thought about me. Then it happened, the unspeakable. On the seventh month, I didn't receive a gift. On the eighth month, I received a gift. Months nine, ten, and eleven, I did not receive a gift, and I was mad at the fact that he got my hopes up in the first six months as if I was going to receive something every month. I was anticipating a gift. I was looking forward to it, yet I was let down. Although he never promised to purchase a gift for me every month, his actions created false expectations. I can't tell you how many businesses I have seen that start out strong— posting every day, engaging the audience—then all of sudden, nothing at all, just like my husband in the above scenario. And two months down the line, they are back as if nothing has happened.

Inconsistency is the first sign of failure in a business. As a matter of fact, in everything. Before you launch a business, think about the good and bad. Ask yourself: Am I built for entrepreneurship? Am I going to be committed to making it work? The worst trait you can have as an entrepreneur is being an indecisive leader. A double-minded man is unstable in all his ways. That's why it's important to be prepared for the journey of entrepreneurship. It takes effort and a strong mindset.

Two people can come from the same background, attend the same school, and be in the same financial situation, and if one of them decides to put forth more effort than the other, guess what the end result will be? The one with the most effort wins. Effort declares you the winner.

Think about the last decision you made to start something new. Whether it's going to college, cleaning out your closet, or losing weight (which seems to always be on the top of my list). You were probably excited about the journey, and as time went by, whether it was for one week or three months, the thrill started to fade and reality sunk in, and like many people you probably asked yourself, "What in the world have I gotten myself into?"

That's how many startup businesses begin the cycle to inconsistency. They start off strong to gain the trust of the market, however, after they make a few dollars, marketing decreases, the owner loses focus and sight of the vision, and the inconsistency starts. Before you know it, that business is added to the list of startups that fail within a few years. I recommend remaining visible to your audience throughout the year even if you have a seasonal business, such as a tax office. You may do less marketing during the offseason, however, consistency keeps you relevant to your clients. Other business owners should establish a 12-month marketing plan and create content that your audience can share with others. Provide relevant information, ask questions, create a hashtag or Facebook business page and/or group and be consistent and plan out the details. As the Master Business Coach & President of The Startup Business Factory, I create my content for the week on Sundays, and post the information I created on a daily basis to stay connected with my audience. Although they may not give me the level of activity or response I desire, when they need my service, they always know where to find me.

Posting, emailing, being active, and engaging your audience is part of marketing. For instance, if a client post on your page or if someone ask a question, it is social etiquette to respond. You may not respond immediately when you receive a notification, but make it a habit of responding to your audience in a timely matter. Others are watching. How does it make you feel when you post or respond on someone's social media page and they don't respond? Put yourself in your client's shoes.

You may not be able to personally respond to each comment or post, but liking it or commenting, in general, is better than not responding at all. When you respond to an individual post, it appears to your social media friends that you are friendly and open to new relationships, which is all part of marketing. Even if a client inboxes you, take the time to respond. You can't have the excuse I don't check my inbox. You have too. Remind yourself how you would like to be treated as a client. Serve your clients and connect with them.

One day I was shopping for my daughter and someone called my name in the store. I spoke although I didn't know the woman nor do I ever remember meeting her in person. Guess where she knew me from? Social media. My short conversation with her solidified our connection. Remember, people don't buy products, they purchase emotions. They buy from you based upon how you make them feel. Social media is about making the person who's reading your post feel a certain way. People actually become your social media friend because they want to know what you like to do outside of business hours. If you're the type of person who doesn't like social media or people, you are limiting your income. I'm not saying you have to be on social media posting all your business, but just share enough to let others know you are personable and relatable.

Now you may be asking, how do I keep it all together as a startup business? How do I stay present and connected with my audience? Good question. There are several recommendations that will help you become consistent.

1. **Time management.** Having too much on your plate at one time causes inconsistency in any area of your life. Plan your day. Your day consists of twenty-four hours, but your time doesn't. Your day starts from the moment you wake up until the moment you lie down. Every second, minute, and hour should be accounted for. You have no time to waste. Wasted time means wasted money. Manage your time, and you'll learn to manage your money and your business.

2. **Schedule your text messages.** Schedule a time throughout the day when you respond to text messages. For instance, I check my text messages three times a day. Morning, noon,

and night. If I check my messages at 10 p.m., which is too late to respond to a client, I can schedule the text message to be sent out the next day. Take advantage of the free tools, such as apps, calendars, and widgets available on your phone to help you become a better business owner.

3. **Write a newsletter.** New business owners tend to rely on social media for communication with their clients. However, newsletters are a great way to connect with your clients consistently. For instance, if you decide to send a newsletter once a month, write twelve newsletters in one day, schedule them for the year, and you're done. Simple, right?

4. **Blogging.** Blogging is a great way to connect with those who may not follow you on social media and who aren't a part of your network. It's a great opportunity for free media exposure. When I wrote money blogs for *Bombshell Magazine*, Founder, and Editor, Nikki Nicole, suggested that we write two to three articles a week. I wrote my articles every Sunday and schedule them to post throughout the week. It doesn't take as long if you stay focused.

5. **Schedule your social media posts**. Hootsuite is a great social media tool that allows you to post on different social media platforms simultaneously to keep your audience engaged. You can also schedule your posts through Hootsuite. I recommend creating contents and scheduling your social media post one week in advance or longer if possible.

These are a few suggested ways to build consistency in your business. Quite frankly, I believe if you're inconsistent in your business, you're probably inconsistent in other areas of your life. I suggest pinpointing one particular area that you've been inconsistent with in your personal life first, work on it. And you will be surprised how one change, will help you to remain focus in your business.

Final Thoughts

Now that you have learned the ten mistakes that startup businesses make, what do you need to do differently in your business? What changes do you need to make? What have you learned that is going to make you a better business owner? Many business owners know what to do, but it takes discipline in order to implement what you've learned.

Being a business owner is hard, and everyone is not cut out to be one. That's why some businesses never make it beyond the startup phase. Your business growth starts with your personal development and implementing what you learn. You will never expand your business further than your knowledge, wisdom, and maturity.

I've said it in Mistake #8, you are your business. It's important that you sharpen the areas in your life that you struggle with the most, such as your attitude and lack of commitment. Being a business owner should make you a better person, but it will also highlight areas of weakness. If you struggle with having a positive outlook on life, it's going to affect your business. If you struggle with wearing your emotions on your shoulder or being sensitive to what people say and/or do, it's going to affect your business. If you struggle with having a negative attitude, it's going to affect your business. Figure out ways to develop as a better person so it won't affect your bank account.

There are several ways to improve yourself:

- **Be around people who intimidate you.** When you are surrounded by people who are smarter and wiser than you, it prompts you to do more.

- **Read self-help books.** Reading is important in business, but reading a self-help book helps you. Read one a month.

- **Take a class.** Even if you aren't religious, spiritual classes help build your morale.

- **Hire a personal development coach.** Entrepreneur, author, and motivational speaker Jim Rohn said it best: "Your level of success will rarely exceed your level of personal development." Personal development coaches are much like life coaches. They specialize in personal growth and overcoming obstacles.

Many times we choose money or choose to work longer hours instead of receiving the help and fine tuning we need to be a personal success in order for our business to reap the benefit. Your business will not outgrow your personal success.

I encourage you to join our free online community for small business leaders to receive training, resources, tips, inspirations and so much more. Type the link below in your web browser (case sensitive) to join The Startup Business Factory, bit.ly/thestartupfb

www.ingramcontent.com/pod-product-compliance
Lightning Source LLC
Chambersburg PA
CBHW060356190526
45169CB00002B/628